SOPHIE FENG

Mind Exhibition

How to Find and Utilize Your Potential

First published by Acorn Row Press 2026

First edition

ISBN: 979-8-9942399-8-8

This book was professionally typeset on Reedsy.
Find out more at reedsy.com

The birth of this book began with the love I received.

Contents

I

Mind Exhibition

1

Intro

We are both museum curators and art admirers.

We organize our life in this museum called the mind with a themed exhibit for each time period in our conscious memories.

Our museum's curator can increase the space for exhibits that showcase subjects and interests that represent who we want. While we may choose to temporarily move or change the topic in current available space, the archive will always remain.

A curator not only analyzes the meaning behind the objects but also the relationship between the present, past, and possible exhibitions. We have to decide on the method in which we present to others and maintain the functionality as well as the museum's clarity. The space should be curated for what you want to keep in the museum - not for people who are not into your art.

The important part of the maintenance is to identify what is the necessary part and the why behind the exhibition. What parts are central to your theme? What are the ultimate accomplishments behind a desire?

To be the curator, you also visit others' museums. The exhibits you are drawn to and are part of will influence you and lead to changes in your museum. Engaging with other people will help you find new pieces or see your curations through curators with other tastes and skills.

How do people see your curations? How are you engaging with other exhibits? How are they changing your curations?

Are you respecting your art or letting others touch it without your consent? Are the people visiting interacting with your hard work in their mind or are they taking your pieces to fill their own greed?

Are you inviting other people to visit or making certain visitors stay because you need them to fill a void?

2

Preview

I became fascinated by the idea that people's thinking can be influenced to subsequently create an infinite number of decisions. Small things make impact beyond what can be analyzed, including the person we choose to become. Changing just one idea can lead to so many other possible paths.

People make actions through their system of thinking strategies. The goal of this guide is to help people become more observant of their patterns and improve their thinking process. Perception shapes the way people think and if the process can be examined, people can see the faster route out of scenarios that aren't the best for their life anymore.

Most times, wounds that we have had, change the future's trajectory. Understanding how, who, why, and what pre-set thoughts can have undesirable consequences in the present will help people make more sensible ideas.

Changing one's thought process has an unlimited potential. The book is to help people be less of a product of others' perspectives and appreciate our individual's characteristics.

There are two purposes for this book. The first one is to hopefully increase people's satisfaction in life by getting to know how to build their potential. I hope it gives people the tools they need to become someone they can and wish to become by being more conscious of their decision making process.

Past events can cause people to act in ways different from who they can be. Self-awareness and willingness to take actions can correct your reactions to external or internal stimuli. Behind an action that links to a pattern is a knot that was formed because of something that you should look into. What is the underlying root change that you faced which caused the creation of the knot? They aren't visible until they are encountered in situations where you are aware of your reactions' patterns.

There is something that caused one to react differently than you. How does your reaction to other people tell yourself what you should work on? By increasing self-awareness level, you can notice how your operating systems can be optimized.

The second reason is the skill of making choices that contribute to one's happiness. To love and to feel love requires skills.

To love others you must learn how to value and love yourself.

3

Exhibit 1: Separate From Other's Projections

Let's talk about the ways to be observant of the knots and their effects by distinguishing people's projections from your reactions.

Is your identity accurate from other people's projections on you? How did other people affect how you see yourself growing up? To undo the knots, you'd need to reflect on the events that shaped you.

Think of your physical and mental wellbeing as if it was a fish swimming in a bowl. Monitor your water level carefully because if it gets to an amount too little, the risk of your fish gasping for air increases. To keep the water level over your fish, ask yourself questions that reflect your state - what decreases or increases your water level?

A friend of mine, P., has the ability to make the people around her feel comforted in her own loving way. She made me feel like

7

as long as I would see her, I would feel better. I feel seen, cared for, and reassured without trying to prove myself. My water supply increases when I'm around her or have conversations with her. Our interactions add water to my water bowl because she values me, provides a safe place where I feel supported, and doesn't make me feel like I am depleting the water supply.

Be an advocate for yourself - How are you doing? Are you feeling okay? To keep your fish under a safe amount of water, save an amount of water for emergency times. Your sense of identity needs to have the freedom to feel unpressured. Make sure your water is enough before you concern yourself with more draining people.

The process of that requires thinking about you and other people's thought systems. Communication is a crucial part to noticing and expressing how you think while taking in information and clues that tell you how other people think.

The skill of seeing the difference between you and others' thought systems gets sharper over time. It is influenced by the people we had growing up, the personal experiences we have, and the ways we reflect on them. In times where individual happiness should matter more than other perspectives, make sure you process your thoughts thoroughly because you have to value your feelings first.

Part of being a good communicator involves speaking out on what you consider inappropriate, disrespectful, and uncomfortable. If someone makes you feel like you need to accommodate them more than they're willing to accommodate you, you have to stand up for yourself in order to prevent them from doing further damage.

Expressing your opinions before your level of water gets below the safety line and setting your pain tolerance to a right point will help you decrease the burden of carrying around unwanted feelings. The way you phrase something is sometimes the key to getting your point across. When you're communicating with someone who you have disagreements with, factor in the associated people's whole backgrounds and thought systems.

Your value is not determined by other people's reactions. People's thoughts are formed based on how they were raised and whether they mean to help or to only think for themselves.

You're more than the projections of you. Your perception of others' projections can also be false. In life, one needs to feel confident first. I hope this book offers some insights to how to get to know yourself, grow potential, and set healthy self-positioning. Change can begin if we become aware of what we lack. Knowing the growth you want to work towards as well as knowing what you don't want is a great starting place!

It's important to be surrounded by people who let you have enough room to be yourself without others' projections of their thought systems onto you. Sometimes it's the people you're associated with that determine how you perceive yourself as.

4

Exhibit 2: Thought System Design

People have a core control center that's set up by what they have experienced in life. The thing is, the programs don't run smoothly if they are rejecting other people from influencing their own programs. Leaving the programs to what they are currently puts their control centers into a less optimized state. Let's say the center can function 100% but not updating its electricity systems reduces the functionality less and less.

The control center can also be damaged by emotions and thoughts that block the electricity conductors. It depends on where the center was broken, the corresponding function reduces or shuts down. The right experiences can reverse the reduced functions to fully functional parts again.

The personalities that we were born with can be changed by the environments that you get placed in. The conductors are fragile. An idea, a few words, a simple action can cause structural changes to the conductors. To stay the state we came in with,

10

you have to exert efforts to maintain the conductors. Even better, you can induce more currents with some alterations to increase the functionality of your panels in the control center.

To check if your panels are as optimized as it can be, you would need stimuli to see your reactions and compare yours with people who are functioning on high efficiency. Which is why you can't be isolated from society. Without them, you won't know what is working and what's not.

If there isn't someone who reminds you of what could have been, it's difficult to realize what the part can look like. Noticing the difference is the first step. Working on the repair is another.

<u>How to Inspect A Thought System</u>: The main source of power is your hope to live. Self-esteem or the confidence to believe you're worthy enough are the backup power that will keep the light on, your positive self-belief, in case the central power shuts down.

We're going to do some inspections on the power source and how to protect and upgrade your panels. Your actions are produced by your thinking processes and your conductors decide what your thinking process is. Who you are today is based on how your conductors are routed that generate your thoughts. So in order to create a system that gives you the reactions you need to turn on your full potential, we need to assess the current conductors and reroute certain ones for your own good.

System Design #1: Decide what codes you want to take in and

be a part of the thought process.

How do you produce what you want? Insert the codes for the product into your system and check if the product is the same as the product you wanted.The codes are how the person you want to learn from thinks and acts. Again, think about if the codes are going to work for you like theirs did. Meaning, are they producing the same outcome or not? Was their situation the same as yours?

If their codes worked due to other factors, will your codes become the product you want to get?

System Design #2: Recognize the codes that fit your needs and replace products that you want to get rid of with codes that would produce the intended results.

A person is the combination of all the codes they have. Without swapping the codes out, your reality won't be able to change because the internal conductor routes are releasing electricity to the wrong directions. Pick the right codes, check if the system is not broken, and set the routes that will lead you to where you want to be.

Our first move is setting goals - become who you want to see. The ideal version of who you are - no, I am not telling you to pretend to be someone else - it's about defining yourself.

5

Exhibit 3: Your Own Projections

It's easy to use only our lens to interpret other people's actions. How you think affects how you take in other people's actions. Is this really how you feel or are they really saying what you think they mean? There are lots of factors that dictate the why behind people's actions such as cultural, education, experience, family dynamics, socioeconomic background, political view, etc. Something someone says can be true for them but doesn't apply to everyone.

Picture each person's lens as a kind of camera equipment. Although your subject is unchanged, the camera uses many factors to take in the view it sees. How much of the picture is it including? How much filter did the photographer use to generate a picture that they want to see instead of the reality? Is the picture in focus or does it not look like the actual scene? What's the photographer's preferences, style, experience? And the context of the why for taking this photograph?

13

The viewer's sensitivity or expertise to the subjects in the photograph on top of one's skills to read beyond the photograph to see the details about the photographer also makes a difference. How much of the actual scenery beyond others' and your individual pictures can the viewer see? Communication and your interactions with others rely on you and others' lenses. What are others' effects on your thought system? How are you influencing theirs? Check your lens' clarity. Are you projecting what you think onto other people? How you feel will confuse your mind into believing that the reaction you perceived is their true intention. Since no two people have the exact same lens, what the other person feels can be different.

Oftentimes, people's ego obstructs their views and their lenses. Seeing and believing only the view you see through your own lens can prevent you from seeing others' views. Being self-confident can motivate you to seek greater achievements. However, too much of it prevents you from seeing reality or other ways out of the situation. Staying open-minded will help you see and communicate more skillfully. It makes it harder to make clear decisions because bias leads people to overestimate or underestimate others and themselves.

Your brain follows thinking patterns that have already been dissected and explored. Many thinking patterns you have. Others have them too. It's important to notice and do more research on your observed patterns. Once you understand more about yours, you'll know how to improve or care for your current panel.

Your thought system is what it is now because of the environment you grew up in and past patterns that you were used to. You have to see others' influence on you. Do you feel like you behave a certain way that some other people don't due to your past? How did other people's actions influence your thoughts?

Looking into sample thinking patterns that are applicable to your life can help you locate the reasons and how you can address the issues you don't want to have anymore. It is inevitable that you will experience events that can help you see the flaws of your thought system. And why you would want to improve it. It might be tempting to focus only on what you could have changed, but it's more important to remind yourself of the growth you have made.

6

Exhibit 4: Self Growth

I magine yourself as a seed. You need to have the right factors to grow: nutrients that can support your growth, space to grow, air, and the right amount of water and sunlight. Are the people you know pushing you to be and do more if you're looking to do that at the moment? Do you feel like your environment has something new to explore?

Having an easy time doesn't mean that you're growing. It's better when you have room to showcase your strengths than not differentiating yourself enough. Using your life as an example. Tailoring it to your likings and needs means giving up what you don't want to fit more of what you want. Taking in everything would be unnecessary. Using your limited resources on what you shouldn't will decrease your chances of being able to say yes to what you want. It's like eating only what you really want and not eating every option on the menu.

Ask yourself what and why you are doing something constantly. Time is your greatest asset. You're not getting it back once it's gone. If something's not building your future or motivating you, it most likely should go. Same thing applies to money, physical, and mental energy.

Save or increase your energy and time with money when you are able to do so. Ideally, protect your long-term happiness by making the things that continue to provide you with new energy. Surround yourself with people who inspire and challenge you to keep growing. Seek growth and learn new things from other people as often as you can. The world is what you think and how you see it. The curiosity of the unknown is the key to having an exciting life.

Pick or create to be in spaces that allow you to enter your brain's flow state, the state of mind which helps you focus. Sometimes you're not the factor. It could be your physical environment, experiences, the people around you, and the opportunities you've had that influenced your seed. Being able to focus deeply is vital.

One way of making the best use out of your attention span is to organize your list of to-do activities by the type of thought function it uses. Putting activities that require a similar thought process such as doing all communication tasks before doing reflective reading would make the switch less time-consuming.

Writing down your thoughts, ideas, and plans gives you a chance to clarify and group them into categories. You can organize your physical environment according to the functions of objects as well. This way your thoughts can be more organized and flow more smoothly.

In addition, be careful of the people who frame you for being the one who made them act that unreasonable, rarely recognize their faults, and make it about themselves. By shifting the false on you, it makes it easier to invalidate how you feel. They like to only count their contribution or even exaggerate and not appreciate the efforts of others.

When interacting with this type, have a strong grasp of the subjective perspective. If you write your side of the situation out, do you see their points as facts or just the opinions that they want you to believe? What do you want to say or do without others' influence? Create the space for making your feelings independent from others' needs and focus on your feelings to give others less influence over you.

Exhibit 5: Potential Exploration

What do you want to see once you have completed life or a project? Think from the end. Then find how you will get there. It's like a business stimulation. You put out a test and see what the feedback sounds like - what needs to be improved? Without figuring out what it is you really want in the end, you might be surprised or even disappointed when you realize that you spent years of your life working towards something you might not even want.

Think through the process- does the process make sense? Many people get caught up wasting time on goals that contribute to their actual goals. Keep in mind that the rewards or results might not meet your expectations. So the process is very important too. Is the process from the beginning to the end what you want? What do you want out of an experience?

In life, the goal, ultimately, is knowing your potential and using it for more than yourself (the hierarchy of needs.)

Simply having enough money without using your potential,

without having enriching social relationships. In other words, without fulfillment is against human nature. So we'll delve into the potential part first then the relationships part in this book.

To know where your innate skills are, you need to examine the reasons behind the decisions that you make. One of the best ways to understand your preferences and predict what you will like is by asking yourself questions.

There are going to be patterns behind why you do the things that you want to do and not because you have to. Think about it like if you were to present your resume with a list with explanations on the stories behind reasons for initiating them and the skills you used on those actions. Hear yourself like an interviewer. What traits or character does this applicant demonstrate?

Questions to ask yourself include:

- Why did I want to do this?
- What interested me in the process?
- What do my skills and efforts mean in the broader sense? How can the skill be used on similar projects that catch your interests?
- Why didn't you pick the other choices?
- How does one experience relate to your past projects? Do you see a pattern emerging from a similar choice logic?
- What do other people say about people who pick this? (Not necessarily all true but you can use them as additional material to consider)
- Are there other options that are closer to your understanding of who you are? Asking others about their opinions on

what you like and dislike could be helpful, but you have to consider if they know you or not.

Your preferences and the skills you want to use more than your other skills become more apparent when you don't expect rewards in return. You wouldn't know your strengths if the people you're surrounded by are not as different from you. That is the reason why you have to pay attention to traits that are unique to you. How would others describe you? Imagine you as a character. What would you do that other supporting roles would say, "That sounds like something [your name] would be great at?"

Put yourself in different quests and teams to activate different skills and test your role when played with diverse players. To write your story that showcases who you are, you should know your potential and the characteristics that make you the character you feel most aligns with yourself. There will be an exploration period because your real self comes out when you don't have to pretend to be someone the world wants to be.

8

Exhibit 6: Fulfillment and Meaning of Life

The meaning of life comes when you don't look for it. It isn't a goal or a job. It can be found after you begin to live in the present and fully enjoy what life has to offer. By enjoying the present, you would naturally gravitate to the things and the people that you find interesting. When you enjoy living, the curiosity to explore the world and discover the world around you, will give you more time to connect to what you are curious about.

Purpose concerns people other than yourself. After all, we are more than individuals. We belong to a greater community. You share the voice of the people in groups that other people identify you as and have shared experiences with. As humans, there are certain experiences and feelings we share all together. You're not the only one who has experienced something. And because strengths can be gained through sharing one's experience. The very existence of you represents a collective hope.

You will be pleasantly surprised about how little you know about the world and get excited to change it. Below is the first partial rough draft of the graduation speech I wrote in high school for an English class. It became the theme of this book.

First Draft:

Living is an accomplishment on its own. Throughout high school, many of us spent countless hours studying to get those As. We strived to be the best students that we could be and hoped that we could get into our dream college. While getting those As is a way of validating ourselves, life is so much more than the grades on our transcripts.

I've come to realize that everything we do, no matter how small or big, has an impact on the history of humankind. Having a fairly unique high school experience taught me that one individual has the potential to impact an unimaginable amount of people. As human beings, we are inevitably influenced by the people around us and the people who we choose to pay attention to on the Internet. Our lives are shaped by their actions and how we choose to respond to those actions.

Living in a society, we play an important role in influencing those around us and those who will hear about you from the people or things that you have influenced. Having gone through distance learning and transitioning back to in-person school, I have truly come to appreciate any kind of human interactions. From small gestures such as waving to a friend to grand gestures like gig birthday presents, I find that the joy of making other people feel seen is what makes my life more than a transcript. Never underestimate the impacts that you can make simply by being yourself.

Every time you talk to another person or put something out on the Internet, you make a permanent mark on someone else's life. While these marks are invisible, it's not difficult to see their impacts. For example, shout out to Ms. K for creating a classroom and creating opportunities for us to get to know each other on a deeper level through countless happiness and crappies, multiple choice groups, and class discussions. Without this class, I would not have the opportunity to learn from each one of you and meet some of my favorite people on the entire planet.

***

This new "speech" is I wish to continue my high school graduation speech with:

The people you meet and the environment we react to change us. During my college years, my perception of self keeps on changing. My sense of self became stronger as I focused on growing the me I hadn't had the chance to meet. I want to share with you the new thoughts that I wish I knew then. With the right people, you will discover your new versions of yourself. The people I met in environments that attracted people with shared characteristics or interests have allowed me to see myself in a new light.

Your perception is more influenced by your feelings than you may think. By changing how you think, you can change how you feel, which will help you act in the way you would prefer more. The impact of our circumstances that shaped us into who we are often is unnoticeable until you react with people who share similar characteristics as you. People who remind you of the person you can be.

You might have trouble seeing yourself clearly sometimes and meeting people with the characteristics that you share will remind you that you have what you see in them too. Having a diverse range of people that you can learn from will complete the blind spots you can't see with your lens. Through exposing yourself to new people, you can know more about your way of thinking or even enrich your worldview.

Since humans' feelings and our thoughts are affected by so many factors. Each person's lens will differ from yours. Try to see from angles that show different scenes of your life in others' lenses. The ability to change how you react can get better with experiences, reflections, and a more optimized thought system.

The world without you wouldn't be the world it is as if you were never born. The people, events, and courses of the future you consciously or subconsciously shaped would not have happened. The changes that you started wouldn't have caused additional ripple changes if you weren't there.

Realizing other people's impact on yourself is the process and taking the steps to change your actions is the next step. I want to thank my family, friends, and the people who believed in me. I was given their time, love, support, among other encouragement resources for my development.

And lastly, I'd like to emphasize that being on your side is how you show yourself kindness. Remember the past and that your perception of your road's scenery is shaping our present.

9

Exhibit 7: How to Find Purpose

Step #1: You need to find what is it that you want to change or improve

It's something you can't help but want to do. Something you can't ignore. Other people don't have as big of a reaction as you. The more you're unsatisfied with the situation, the more satisfied you will be when you have corrected it. If you don't already know what it is, go somewhere you normally aren't in. Meet new people who bring out different and new sides that you haven't been aware of.

When the right event occurs, you'll react bigger and that's how you will find the answer.Overtime, there should be a theme in the reactions that you have had.

*　*　*

Step #2: Analyze your natural abilities and character from the time you spent on doing what you're interested in

For each activity you initiated (the key here is you reacted to and attempted to change the situation), write a paragraph about what the push factor was (that shows why you wanted to do it) and what skills were used. This way, you will see patterns of your characteristics and interests). There will be themes behind your actions. Each should point to a broad inclination that can be used in other activities.

As an example, a pattern I had was building something that bridges the resource gap. I wanted to close the discrepancies between people. To do this, I started a club in high school to translate documents to other languages so students' parents who can't understand them will be able to participate in their children's school lives.

More examples that formed a pattern from this was the idea I had of compiling the schools' resources into a packet or a hub where students would have more access and awareness of the opportunities available to them. In high school, the idea was a packet, and a few years later, in college, it evolved into creating a hub online that people can post about their experiences at a specific dorm, class, or club. People in different majors can post the classes they have taken and extracurriculars they have done. This way, people who are interested in doing similar career pathways can be more sure of what they're interested in. And now, I am sharing what I learned in my life that I think can help other people through this book.

The same pattern was apparent since I was little but you get the point. Analyze the repetitive patterns: what was the same about the intention behind doing a passion project and what does that say about the way you are.

* * *

Step #3: Know what your light bulbs are

What makes you think more and feel more? Sometimes you won't know how different your thoughts are unless you are aware of the people who don't think like you. Your background and experience have shaped your interests and skills to a unique set of light bulbs that get lit up in times of reacting with the light bulbs that have overlapping characteristics, personality, skills, interests, and passions.

These lights are the outward parts of your panels. Conductors that are covered by external factors dim certain light bulbs from their achievable brightness. Interacting with other light bulbs that correspond to the areas that are hidden away can make you realize what you want to improve.

You might think you connect to people who have similar thought processes or share some light bulbs with you. Experiences you go through alter your panel's conductors in patterns that you may be able to spot in other people with shared experiences. Observing what you have in common will help you understand yourself.

However, people sharing overlapping similarities don't necessarily have the same thinking processes. Reasons including but not excluding self-esteem, values, cultural, economic, and social background all influence how one thinks. Liking the same things doesn't make two people complementary to each other. You might also feel connected to someone because you think you see the solutions to the optimization of your thought system's conductors in them. But it might be that you're projecting your feelings onto them. Another possible explanation is that you see part of yourself through them.

In addition, the light bulbs that you don't like mostly contradict the ones you like. What do you dislike? What type of situations make you react the most? The reactions' underlying reasoning is mostly related to what you care a lot about. Ask yourself what you don't want when considering the possible choices you are thinking about. What do you absolutely not want?

Keep in mind that how you feel changes with experience and time. You need to distinguish what catches your interest the most out of the available lit up light bulbs. If you are caught between options, decide where, who, and what you're willing to spend more resources on. Think through the process and the possible reasons why you would like or hate doing something. You can enjoy some specific parts of the project but not exactly the whole project. List out the aspects that you like and don't like about the projects you have done. You can test which one you are more interested in by trying to hate the choice you think you want or by comparing your characteristics to people who have enjoyed the process.

To summarize the steps: Identify what your reasons are behind doing or choosing an option, then know what factors would keep you going, lastly set up potential opportunities where you are given similar jobs and responsibilities. Would you want to take it if there was no compensation? Take low-time commitment projects to test your theory, delve deeper, understand your personality first and then cross off what doesn't fit.

The core question is I would love to meet [the kind of people] because I think I would want to have [traits]. Doing what fulfills your heart is more important than what is not as personal to you because your potential can ideally make a positive impact on what you care about. Purpose has to be something that extends from what you are passionate about and who you want to present yourself as.

What would you want to be able to do and talk about? Would you want to include it in your exhibit as your curation?

Exhibit 8: Strategies to Find Potential

Potential needs to be highlighted. In its rawest form, it may not appear obvious but if you spend time growing it and are determined to do something out of it, eventually, the potential will be something invaluable. Lots of factors can affect the growth rate of your potential. Place yourself in situations that will make you utilize skills that you normally don't use. The goal of this is to find the skills that you pick up faster than other people.

Think about how you are able to create values that many people can benefit from. What can you offer that other people find helpful that you also enjoy as it aligns with your purpose? Remember, your job is to prove your authentic self.

It's truly a wonderful feeling to know there are people with different skills than you. Let others help you with what you are less talented at and use your talents to benefit other people. Imagine what would happen if everyone was born with the same skill sets and raised in the same way. Together with other people, we can make the world filled with experiences that are much more specialized.

If you can find that one thing or multiple things that you do more easily than many others and find it enjoyable, I would assume that it would make sense to pursue that. If each person finds what they do best and pursues that, the world will have more advancements and people who are better at what they do.

Just because the people you are surrounded by can't recognize your talents, it doesn't mean you don't have them. Potential is like a seed hidden in the mix with other soil ingredients. Your ability to spot that is key. Meet new groups of people and put your skills to use and you'll begin to identify it.

The unknown can be hard to predict but staying in predictable environments hinders growth. The reactions that propel growth have to be stimulated through overcoming obstacles. Staying inside what you have known limits the amount of stimuli that produce new reactions. The more you do what you like, the more you'll have to analyze because it will get easier to point out patterns that show your characteristics.

You can be good at a lot of things but choose to do what brings you the most happiness. Stop if something doesn't inspire you or make you want to do even better. Not everything should be 'productive' - rest time is crucial. New ideas are created through explorations and experiments with different combinations of stimuli.

Being the owner of your life makes you responsible to build it as well as you can. How do you use your available resources to get to where you want to be? You have to track your investments - in all aspects - to avoid wasting your resources as they are limited. Time for the most part - attention span, the time you have to rest, eat, time to get to places, and interact with people - do a selection of what should stay and what you should let go of.

Keep in mind that you shouldn't shorten the time you use to explore yourself, going to places that inspire or rejuvenate you, or from spending time with friends and family members. Activities that inspire you to work towards your dreams and rejuvenate your mind, spirit, and health should be kept and adjusted to fit into schedule.

Try to be in places that have the resources to help you grow into who you want to be. Be willing to invest in opportunities and changes that would bring you more in the long run. For example, upgrade the equipment you use to be more efficient to get more time to focus on your tasks. Counterintuitively, audit your life every now and then. Try to go a few days or a few weeks without something. Maybe you would like your life better if you have or do certain things less or even none at all.

11

Exhibit 9: Stay Cautious

Consider the favors they do to gain your trust, it's not your responsibility to return them anything. Ask and make your decisions based on enough reliable information. Be careful you're a special circumstance that other people are claiming you to be. Check if they are making a correct argument or claim first or not. Try to separate your fear to process your thoughts more clearly but still listen to your intuition though.

When facing choices that you think will solve a task, think how much you're letting others influence how much you believe in your ability or yourself. Check a considerable number of sources before you make a choice to seek someone's help for something you can accomplish on your own without their advice. By saying that if you turn to them, things would be a lot faster or easier, ask what their motive is. Who are the target audience and who aren't? Why would you not work with them? Do you see why other people have trust issues with this event or person?

35

If they say they normally don't do it (if you're an exception), that they're doing you a special favor, or trying to prevent you from contacting others who may disagree with their perspectives, be even on higher alert. If someone were trying to do you a favor, they won't sound as if you have to work with them. A big giveaway for suspicious activity is if they don't want you to tell others and/or ask you to say something other than what you're doing. Validate their claims' legitimacy by researching and checking other potential solutions. Urgency and fear make people think illogically sometimes. Calm down first, remember that you likely have more time than you think to process, then decide.

If you're hesitant or have questions, pause and ask. Rather than should and shouldn't, choose to do the choice that makes you confident and looking forward towards. You don't have to go with something if you don't want to. You can take a less popular route because you're the one who gets to choose the outcome of your decision and lives with it.

When you feel like a solution is too complex for an uncomplicated problem, doubt it and find the insight you are probably missing. Something can be wrong about it. Similarly, if a complicated problem is being presented as a very simple one, it might be a sign that it's orchestrated to appear the way it is, so make sure to do your research. Question why they said something or asked for something especially if sensitive details are involved. Do they sound too confident, too nonchalant, or too reassuring?

People who are trying to trick you may sound as if they were taking you for granted. Too little or too much care is another sign. Mixing what you believe with what they want you to believe is an easy way to tell what someone's true intentions are. Why didn't they and why they did certain things are questions you should keep in mind when encountering unsure situations. What would they benefit by doing this? Who are they trying to be? There can be factors that cause humans to act in ways that do not necessarily show their real feelings or motives.

People often treat the people in their lives differently depending on the amount of trust they have for that person. The important point is don't overestimate the trust level you are at in someone's trust bank. Be conscious about the amount of trust you let someone build up in your bank. Placing the wrong level of trust (either more or less) can cause losses that may be emotional, monetary, etc.. Having appreciation for others and understanding what you don't want are equally important.

You can tell a lot about people through knowing what they care about in life. If someone has already shown you that they're not someone you should trust, be wary of their actions. Generally speaking, people one surrounds themselves with can tell you a lot about who they are. Who are they close to? People's values can change depending on one's life experiences so check once in a while if a person becomes connected to people you shouldn't trust.

Thinking from a business point of view can provide more clarity. Emotions can be formed based on perceived circumstances and how you feel can change, but facts are hard to dispute.

Don't let emotions interfere with the fact people will see and create problems that emotion can't amend.

At different periods of your life, there are different responsibilities, worries, and desires. Every turn has a big impact on your life. Think through the factors that impact the short-term, long-term potential loss or addition to social, physical, and other important aspects of your life.

12

Exhibit 10: Social Life

To love means wanting to treasure them and to protect them. The people you love are what you want to keep safe, to hope to flourish. The thumb rule is: they want you to do well. Time wise, energy wise, feelings wise, money wise, they are willing to help you grow. Depends where they are coming from. People who want you to become capable of taking care of yourself will interfere and offer help like advice or suggestions for improvement.

Imagine each person has an invisible feeling temperature detector. When they're used to a certain way of getting treated, their detector's measurement system will be used to that kind of condition. People from all across have different temperature settings. Their thought systems affect their perception as well.

Check that your detector doesn't have an incorrect measurement detector. And know that sometimes your detector and others' won't sense the same temperature the same way. What is the temperature they're used to sensing? How does your

39

relationship affect how the temperature detectors work for you and other people involved? To feel in the temperature measurement system that fits you the best, you'd examine the current detector's status then adjust the measurements correlated interpretations.

If the other person likes food A, don't give them food B unless food A is bad for them. The love you want to give has to be what they want. And try not to overextend the amount of love you want to give. For example, you have 100 beads. Giving one to someone doesn't make you want something in return. On the contrary, if you give someone 50 beads, then of course you will feel like you are giving a lot and they should compensate you.

The right kind of love can make you so much stronger and the wrong kind can cause you to lose focus in life. Your story is yours. Think about the interactions you would have with someone. Are they someone you want to share time together with? When you both enter a story line, how does their part change who you are? Will it go the way you like? The developments need to be positive. Your dominant traits and their dominant characteristics shouldn't be in contrast. More importantly, how do they react to your stronger traits? The differences in your thoughts now will be increased with the number of decisions you have to make in the future.

People who don't care about your feelings are those who really don't value you. You are seen as someone not as valuable to them. If they truly valued you, how would they treat you? Think about the differences from this comparison' point of view. They can be fooling themselves too. Sometimes they want to believe that they care but base your decision on the facts. While there may be situations that get confusing but if they care, they will be mindful about your perspective.

Some people see themselves through the same lens they use to see themselves. How people think of themselves will get projected to how they think of you. If they are judgmental towards themselves, they will likely judge you too. If they are not a hard worker themselves, they will think not working hard is okay for you as well. How they think about others is a good indicator of how they will think of you eventually. The lens one sees others and the world is the lens they're going to use on you. If you think you're an exception, you're likely wrong. The difference can be temporary due to factors that are like emotions, perceived information, and etc.

People's feelings change more constantly than their thought system does. It is hard to change it unless they're willing to hear other voices. Therefore, pick who you are associated with carefully. Make sure that you're clear about their boundaries and vice versa. Things happen and people's feelings can get hurt if the boundaries don't align. The earlier you can tell the differences, the better.

13

Note from the Curator

When you are looped into a thought spiral, observe what can cut it in a half. Think about what paradoxically observation would kill the set up of the scenario itself. This type of thinking offers a cross-check to the question and examines the rationality and believability of it.

Make sure to pay attention to your subconscious thoughts. How you interact with the objects, emotions, and people you're surrounded with - sometimes the friends you think you need don't deserve you. One thing that I realized is that when a person isn't making you feel respected or cares about your genuine wellbeing, your friendship will likely come to an end.

There are people who will meet the standard to show how deserving and valuable it is to have you in their life. Don't question your worth for people who under appreciate or are jealous of you and try to bring you down with them. Healthy relationships can be hard to have but those who value you, encourage you in general, are there for you, and can enjoy each other's presence are worth it.

When you care about someone, it is most likely that your emotions become more vulnerable. Humans express their needs in many different forms. The reasons behind people's actions, including how you are viewed, are tied to their needs and personal backgrounds. Differences between others and you are shared characteristics, not only yours, so depending on who or the events that change your perception and theirs, not everyone can get along.

The significance or the unique features of a certain artwork needs to be recognized by the viewers who appreciate it. Placing a valuable artwork in a place where no one values it only means they aren't your audience.

The light others see you is a reflection of their lights. If a particular audience has a different taste or isn't trained to understand the type of art you are, your value may not be accurately evaluated.

Art as a person changes around the situation it's around. Therefore, if you haven't found the audience appropriate for you, think about the people you're surrounded by or the place you are in. An interactive art depends on both people - the concept is how someone treats you most likely reveals who they are - an art doesn't lose value just because a person can't have the time or taste to adore it.

Being in a familiar dynamic requires a lot of courage and

boundary separation to be reminded of how certain social relationships can be healthier and that you deserve to be happy too.

The strength to grow and be who you want to be - not who you have to be - will set you free.

The habits that have become natural and part of your everyday routine might not necessarily be what you should keep. For your "considered" strong characteristics, what if you treat them like wounds?

Are you doing it out of need or past pattern? One thing I want to close the book with is to hand over the spotlight you use on the people you love to others.

Remember you are perceived through the lenses of cameras with backstories that you don't completely understand. Is your perception influenced by others? If your perception of yourself was tied to the people around you, did those people like you? Sometimes we can't make a decision that truly makes us happy if we don't consider how we feel.

My experience with people has shown me that if someone genuinely cares and loves you, they make sure that you understand they care about you. What type of love are you letting your friends or romantic interest express on you? How are you showing self-love to yourself? The right puzzle pieces are the complimentary joy of becoming your higher re-programmed self.

14

Author's Words

There are many negative lenses you might end up seeing the world in. But I hope you remember to notice that you have the ability to discover the positive lenses as well. Being someone who is gently held, I think, is a feeling I have learned from being associated with others. Be aware of how you act and how you think about others - it changes your relationships with the world.

The importance of truly knowing your thought process is so that you get to find your true self and have fulfilling social relationships. In my opinion, becoming aware of the blind spots in your thoughts will give you a higher interest in life and a more meaningful way of life.

Finally, I hope you can surround yourself with the people who see you and expand your love for not only your life, but also others' lives. If you have been truly accepted and loved by a friend, family, or lover, that kind of caring love can overflow your heart and inspire you to care more with more purpose.

I hope that you have a working detector of what kind of love you want to give or take. The kind where you're happily in, with others and yourself. Who loves and cares so much about you and to have meals with people who make your food more flavorful with their presence. A very delightful friend who you simply enjoy being around in life.

15

Track 1-4

Track 1: Mood

I originally intended for the book to be listened to in one's room alone at night. The imagination first came when I lived off-campus. When the sky turns dark, you're the only person in the room - I find solitude and moments of quiet in life extremely rare.

*****

Track 2: The Choices:

Choices compound. What I choose not only changes my life but people who are affected by my life or will. Those then go on and influence the people who they know of. The chain of influence continues through a web of choices and our lives can change through a single decision.

What factors play in the decision processes that can alter paths? Choices can be very difficult to break down. People's minds are delicate and intricate. But, I believe the chances of making happy choices can be influenced. And which is what I'm aiming to increase through creating a thought system that would produce more fulfilling outcomes.

* * *

Track 3: Finding A Balance:

At a certain turning point in your life, it's natural to start thinking that you have done enough. You have to be ready to choose yourself when you can't afford keeping some people in your circle. You deserve people worthy enough of your heart and value your gifts.

When facing people who love themselves to the extent where you are paying for their choices, take their ecosystem into the story. What one receives, takes, and builds from one's available resources changes how they interact with their world.

* * *

Track 4: Measuring Love:

Loving someone gives them the love one can fill their self-love needs with. Love comes with different strings attached from family and other social circles.

Imagine the love you hold for yourself and for the world are placed in two bowls and put on a balance. When the love you give is greater than the mass of self-love, you will feel like you're not trying hard enough.

Self-understanding is the root of appreciation for oneself. Admiration and protection are keys to pouring water in your fish bowl. Seeing the water level of other people will save many from blaming oneself over others' emotions. Sometimes, the other party's bowl is unable to pour into your relationship. In those situations where they are using you to get the water needed to keep their happiness without caring about your fish, remember to take care of your fish.

* * *

16

Track 5-9

Track 5: Love Quality

It turns out that the people who love me try to make me feel heard. There's a need-type of love that happens when someone needs you to like them to make themselves feel better.

* * *

Track 6: Mutual Support

Being cherished for being your true self - both accepted and valued - is one of the most beneficial and important factors when you're deciding on the people you want to love. There's a fundamental difference between the people whose presence will encourage you and those who make you feel as though you're spending extra effort to stay. We shouldn't try overly hard to keep something because we have to move on to continue to be ourselves.

By brushing off our own feelings, we get engulfed by the shades of our emotions.

* * *

Track 7: Struggle to Support

I first wanted to thank myself for not listening to the remarks of some unsupportive people.

Why can't I think like the biggest observer of my movie and root for myself?

What do the scenes in my plot line show me about who I really want to be and develop into my role? How does my information about me change the direction I'm headed?

* * *

Track 8: Planning Outline (August 2024):

The book is organized into three phases. The first phase helps readers identify what would make them happy in the long-run; their unique strengths, weaknesses, passions, and purpose; implements a business mindset that would help them be more effective and efficient in life.

The second phase transitions from discussing self to other people. It includes strategies to create meaningful social relationships; ways of predicting someone's actions in addition to what readers can do to prevent certain interactions; examinations to find hidden limitations in readers' minds that cause them to fail and how to resolve them.

The last phase aims to help readers build up confidence and restore hope when they encounter unpleasant experiences with personal anecdotes and principles. It also ends the book with reiterations of my points.

* * *

Track 9- Your Story, Only You

Isn't it satisfying to see that your happiness is because of you? The process began to become easier as soon as I stopped worrying about whether other people will like me and simply write what I am drawn to.

Most times, we want to be the protector of the people and things we cherish, but am I actually helping or am I doing them a favor by sacrificing my happiness?

I know it can be hard to accept the truth but the people you should love should love you back. If they stop being someone who you love or don't have the will to take care of your love, it's because they aren't the people who can stay in your story anymore.

Your story line has a different focus than theirs- from your priorities, values, characters, and type of person you want to become. It's because your direction is not the one they can go with you.

17

Track 10-14

Track 10: The Cure

The people you meet can change the way you live life. What seemed to break the numbness was forcing myself to commit to a goal and enjoying the excitement of achieving something I was proud of.

What really helped me was having someone, a friend, who I knew wanted to be my company. Someone who simply sat next to me, accepted me, and truly saw me.

* * *

Track 11: Focus

The key is shifting the time and attention you center on yourself to others. In other words, put others in mind and change the setting on your love detector. This way, you would be more skilled at being loved and loving others.

* * *

Track 12: Self Reserve

There is a possibility of unconsciously playing a character's role you have become in circumstances beyond your wish. The effort you put in to satisfy other people's needs could be suppressing your true self. In this case, you have to make yourself more unavailable and lower your expectation for outside acclamation.

By decreasing the air supply other people regularly give you, you increase the efficiency of the air supply builder in your own mind. This will make your self-value reserve have a bigger amount when in comparison to your need to satisfy the people you love.

The people you love can't drain your reserve whether knowingly or unknowingly. You have the right to call it out - those requests are likely made by unreasonable bank clients.

* * *

Track 13- Supply of Air

Depression is putting yourself into a space with a scarce amount of air. You can't let the weight of the bubble around it take up the air in your room. Try to find your methods of decreasing the size of the bubble.

What helped me has been promising people that I will try to take care of myself and expose myself to a new environment even if I prefer to stay inside. When I was not sleeping or eating healthily, my close friends and family would express concerns.

When you have people who really want you to be good to yourself, including yourself specifically, you'll most likely want them to feel less worried. If it's going to take time to heal then I'll remember to continue making myself feel loved, looked after, and cared for.

Interacting and talking to people will somewhat offset the air being suffocated by the bubble. The key is to increase the air in the space to stop the bubble.

If going somewhere is too much, lower your expectations. You don't need to achieve a goal. Any type of improvement is worth the effort. When you put yourself in different settings and with different people, the change will expose you to objects that remind you how good it is to feel alive.

* * *

Track 14- The Reflection

I learned that I have to love the fact that I exist to love other people. If I can't love myself wholeheartedly, then I can't love other people that I want because I can't give beyond the love for myself.

Being loved is to receive the feeling of having been taken care of by someone who understands who you are and pays attention to in a nourishing way.

18

Bonus Track: Choosing Happiness

The question- what really makes us happy- often pops into my head. I think that we have to want to be fulfilled. When there is a choice to choose happiness, don't choose unhappiness. It might seem obvious but it may not be.

The patterns that increase happiness won't work unless you follow them. Does this action fit into your happiness or will result in one's happiness? I recommend that you identify the people who would choose to let you be immersed in happiness.

19

Outro.

Happiness is being around memories and planets that make your planet grow its mass. After everything I discussed, I hope you get to choose to do what makes life feels exciting and worth looking back to.

II

Recording Diaries

20

Memory Storage

This writing process was me organizing the curation I've learned and presenting my experiences into an exhibit for other people through this book.

We store our memories in people and associate our feelings with certain pictures, songs, places, movies, words, texture, color, etc..

The writing journey brought me to museums that show exhibitions of who I was and would like more in my museum. I took out items on display and exposed myself to what I want to own.

The removing, browsing around the world (the Internet as well) for the new space, adding the new to the museum, reorganizing old exhibits to make the exhibit flow increases or decreases the mass of your planet.

When a memory brings you back to a particular moment, the piece of time along with the elements that encapsulates your history. And it gets to be enjoyed with people despite time.

Our lives interact with other people's museums. The books, shows, paintings, and any piece of history's results we see, feel, hear, or even taste can be accessed by people through creations and simply being who we are.

21

Development Takes Time

Seeds take time to grow and mature. The first draft of this book had to take a year to become the latest edition and the idea of the books took many years to take shape. Just like my writing timeline, life is full of time periods like those periods of connecting ideas.

The Seed(December 2024):

Becoming who I wanted to become was the echoing dream of my teenage years. On the journey to adulthood, I have met people with whom I only had a very short amount of time with. I might not have had the opportunity to say how much I cherished those moments then but thank you for being kind and compassionate.

Growing Seed(November 2025):

I think self-worth is like the mass of someone's planet. The greater the mass is, the greater the gravitational pull becomes. Thus, grounding you from other planets' forces.

22

Intertwined

A direction change can result in the positive impact on countless new galaxies. Thus, your decisions are influencing the paths of the current existing planets and the journeys they inspire.

23

Letter

I know sometimes it's not easy to believe that going with the information you have will work out. Although uncertainty can be intimidating, letting things unfold naturally will leave some room for these unplanned people and surprising revelations.

Give yourself more self-understanding and empathy to support yourself so when other people fail to see it, you can still prevent the sadness and frustrations stemming from those root causes.

The more you understand and allow yourself to support yourself, the more you can love others and yourself.

24

The Speech Ending

The ending to the high school graduation speech I gave in my English class:

Throughout high school and beyond we are going to find ourselves encountering numerous obstacles. There will be times when you think that no one else understands your struggles. Please always remember that there are about 7.7 billion people in this world and someone out there understands or has gone through similar experiences as you. You can and should reach out to the world in times of despair because no one can do it alone. As we leave high school behind and take on the real world, don't forget that you are born with the skill to influence the world. Congratulations Class of 2022 - we did it!

III

The Opening Gala

25

Events

To start the gala, our first event is to be able to realize someone's character. What you should ask yourself is why you are close with this person. The question you should ask is how would they affect your relationship both positively and negatively.

When a social relationship disconnects, where do you see yourself afterwards? Is the world we see similar or different? Do I want my friends to do this to me or is this something I would be sensitive to if you were not close to me?

If it doesn't work, is this someone with enough integrity? It is what will be left when there isn't a connection and you're not their friend. Is there enough mutual understanding that you're willing to be okay with?

The next event is deservingness or what you feel comfortable with. Is it healthy? The idea that you deserve what may be unfamiliar to you even though you may be new to that.

Sometimes people don't know they can and should be treated with attention and care.

The following event is you need to know what decisions will make you excited. When you're choosing something, think only about what happens as a result of your decision without the parts you like. Some overlook the long-term or lasting effect when the short-term effect seems ideal. Although immediate gratification may bet tempting, it's the long-term result you'll live with.

Next, we have mismatching pairings. You may be a professional but if the other party is only a beginner, the game outcome will largely depend on the collaboration. Therefore, the pairing is a two-person team. If you experience pairing problems, who is influencing the result?

At last, the quality of a social connection is seen in times of vulnerabilities. How similar you and their traits are will show you the compatibility of your worldviews. However, to truly see each other, you have to know the way each other reacts to vulnerabilities.

What I have observed is that the deeper you can bare your soul to someone, the deeper your connection will be. The people who prioritize their joy without thinking of you are not your real friends. Communication requires you to understand different perspectives which I hope the album is able to help you become more experienced at.

26

Speech

A lot of choices many people make are to decrease disappointment. What would disappoint you?

It's the stem of the important patterns that shape you.

When you make a decision, think about what would not compromise your heart. Do you have to convince yourself to make the decision and is that your choice because you want to?

There can be suppressed patterns that you have learned to help you in the past but are blocking your expression.

My friend, P., warms me up so much that I feel like she pulled me out of the pond and wrapped a blanket around me. I love being near her because she's a fire pit for my heart. What I am trying to say is being around the people who warm you and connect with you well is essential.

Generally, the closer your views get and support each other in ways the other party desires, the easier it is to build a relationship with them. When your views aren't the same, you have to pay attention to the impact the differences can have on the connection. The separation begins with a contrast that creates a confusion. There are fundamental worldview conflicts under the tiny contrast in your behaviors.

This book is my wish to help people grow from and out of the environment we were shaped by. We have the power to alter the world pre-built for us and build our own mind. Every brick of your thought castle is a piece in the puzzle that plays a role in your past and in the present.

If you observe your present and your thought system's shape, you will be able to support yourself. Through understanding your choices, you will also have a deeper awareness of others' reasons behind their choices. Thus, increasing your chances of resonating and immersing yourself with what you resonate with.

I believe it's important to be able to have a well-coded thought system and preserve subjectivity even when interacting with others. As well as having a system that can hopefully lead you to making the choices you are satisfied with.

27

Visiting Artist

By sharing my thoughts with other people, I have become friends with the people I'm fortunate to have shared similar reflections with.

Those reflections and visiting their exhibitions have greatly influenced my curations. As an example, a friend of mine's exhibitions have been very comforting as her words are filled with light. She is someone I would love to reflect and share my mind with. So I want to tell you I am proud to have been influenced by many inspirational exhibitions and their light bulbs of memories.

I hope this work heals you or at the very least improves your healing system. Most urgently your love level and perspective of yourself.

28

Closing Notes

Music Taste:

It takes skills and practices to express your care. The work takes the person who expresses their thoughts as well as the person who is listening to be understood. When making choices, think what music pieces you want to take a part of.

Belief:

I hope that you believe in unlikely but possible chances. Hard to believe results exist and may shock people, even yourself. After all, we want a life that is worth remembering and where our actions change the world.

Acknowledgments

I have to start with my family- I'm so fortunate to have them in my life. Thank you for loving me.

I've always loved the person I could be with my friends. I have received help from more people than I can include but I would like to thank these people here specifically: AK, Ayesha, BC, Cindy, Jessica, Jolene, Karen, Mia, Michelle, Patricia, Solbi, Sophia, Tara, and Terry.

Lastly, to America Writers Museum for opening my eyes to writers' impact.

About the Author

Sophie Feng's an immigrant who grew up in Taiwan and Los Angeles. She had an online business and managed three assistants when she was a high school junior. She realized that fulfillment comes from utilizing and developing potential in life. After graduating from high school in 2022, she attended the University of Washington and New York University in hopes of finding a systematic way of increasing fulfillment. After her second year, she began working on this book full-time and finished writing in one and a half years.

You can connect with me on:
🌐 https://sophiefenging.com

www.ingramcontent.com/pod-product-compliance
Lightning Source LLC
Chambersburg PA
CBHW010322180726
47991CB00022B/3168